MW01268804

SYRINGA VULGARIS - THE COMMON LILAC SPECIES

DESCRIPTION

Syringa vulgaris, commonly known as the common lilac or French lilac, is a deciduous shrub that can grow up to 20 feet tall. It has heart-shaped leaves and produces fragrant, showy panicles of flowers in shades of purple, pink, white, and blue in the spring.

ORIGIN AND DISTRIBUTION

Syringa vulgaris is native to the Balkan Peninsula in southeastern Europe. It has been widely cultivated in Europe and North America for its ornamental value and is now naturalized in many parts of the world.

CULTIVATION

The common lilac prefers full sun to partial shade and well-drained soil. It is hardy in USDA zones 3 to 7 and can be propagated by cuttings or by seed. Pruning should be done after flowering to maintain its shape and promote new growth.

USES

Syringa vulgaris is primarily grown as an ornamental plant for its beautiful flowers and fragrance. It is also used in traditional medicine for its astringent and anti-inflammatory properties. The flowers can be used to make a variety of products such as perfumes, soaps, and essential oils.

SYRINGA PUBESCENS - A CHINESE NATIVE LILAC WITH WHITE OR PINK FLOWERS

DESCRIPTION

Syringa pubescens, commonly known as the Chinese lilac, is a deciduous shrub that typically grows up to 10 feet tall. It has glossy, dark green leaves and produces fragrant, small panicles of flowers in shades of white or pink in the spring.

ORIGIN AND DISTRIBUTION

Syringa pubescens is native to China and can be found growing in mountainous regions in central and western China. It has been cultivated in Europe and North America for its ornamental value.

CULTIVATION

The Chinese lilac prefers full sun to partial shade and well-drained soil. It is hardy in USDA zones 3 to 7 and can be propagated by cuttings or by seed. Pruning should be done after flowering to maintain its shape and promote new growth.

USES

Syringa pubescens is primarily grown as an ornamental plant for its beautiful flowers and fragrance. It is a popular choice for landscaping and can be used as a hedge, border plant, or specimen plant. The flowers can also be cut and used in floral arrangements.

SYRINGA PATULA - A DWARF KOREAN LILAC WITH PINKISH-LAVENDER FLOWERS

DESCRIPTION

Syringa patula, commonly known as the dwarf Korean lilac, is a deciduous shrub that typically grows up to 6 feet tall. It has small, dark green leaves and produces fragrant, small panicles of flowers in shades of pinkish-lavender in the late spring to early summer.

ORIGIN AND DISTRIBUTION

Syringa patula is native to Korea and can be found growing in rocky areas and mountain slopes. It has been cultivated in Europe and North America for its ornamental value.

CULTIVATION

The dwarf Korean lilac prefers full sun to partial shade and well-drained soil. It is hardy in USDA zones 3 to 7 and can be propagated by cuttings or by seed. Pruning should be done after flowering to maintain its shape and promote new growth.

USES

Syringa patula is primarily grown as an ornamental plant for its beautiful flowers and fragrance. It is a popular choice for small gardens, borders, and rock gardens. The flowers can also be cut and used in floral arrangements.

SYRINGA X HYACINTHIFLORA - A HYBRID LILAC WITH LARGE, FRAGRANT, LAVENDER-PINK FLOWERS

DESCRIPTION

Syringa x hyacinthiflora, commonly known as the hyacinth lilac, is a deciduous shrub that can grow up to 12 feet tall. It has dark green leaves and produces large, fragrant, lavender-pink flowers in the late spring to early summer.

ORIGIN AND DISTRIBUTION

Syringa x hyacinthiflora is a hybrid between Syringa vulgaris and Syringa oblata. It was developed in France in the early 20th century and has since been widely cultivated in Europe and North America for its ornamental value.

CULTIVATION

The hyacinth lilac prefers full sun to partial shade and well-drained soil. It is hardy in USDA zones 3 to 7 and can be propagated by cuttings or by layering. Pruning should be done after flowering to maintain its shape and promote new growth.

USES

Syringa x hyacinthiflora is primarily grown as an ornamental plant for its beautiful flowers and fragrance. It is a popular choice for landscaping and can be used as a hedge, border plant, or specimen plant. The flowers can also be cut and used in floral arrangements.

SYRINGA MEYERI - A COMPACT CHINESE NATIVE LILAC WITH FRAGRANT PURPLE OR PINK FLOWERS

DESCRIPTION

Syringa meyeri, commonly known as Meyer lilac, is a deciduous shrub that typically grows up to 6 feet tall. It has small, glossy leaves and produces fragrant clusters of purple or pink flowers in the late spring to early summer. The plant is known for its compact size and rounded growth habit.

ORIGIN AND DISTRIBUTION

Syringa meyeri is native to China and was introduced to the United States by Frank Meyer in the early 1900s. It has since been widely cultivated for its ornamental value and can be found growing in gardens and landscapes throughout North America and Europe.

CULTIVATION

The Meyer lilac prefers full sun to partial shade and well-drained soil. It is hardy in USDA zones 3 to 7 and can be propagated by cuttings or by layering. Pruning should be done after flowering to maintain its shape and promote new growth.

USES

Syringa meyeri is primarily grown as an ornamental plant for its beautiful flowers and compact size. It is a popular choice for small gardens, borders, and rock gardens. The flowers can also be cut and used in floral arrangements.

SYRINGA JOSIKAEA - A HUNGARIAN NATIVE LILAC WITH PINK OR PURPLE FLOWERS

DESCRIPTION

Syringa josikaea, commonly known as the Hungarian lilac, is a deciduous shrub that can grow up to 10 feet tall. It has dark green leaves and produces clusters of pink or purple flowers in the late spring to early summer. The plant is known for its upright growth habit and attractive bark.

ORIGIN AND DISTRIBUTION

Syringa josikaea is native to Hungary and surrounding areas of eastern Europe. It has been cultivated for its ornamental value and can be found growing in gardens and landscapes throughout Europe and North America.

CULTIVATION

The Hungarian lilac prefers full sun to partial shade and well-drained soil. It is hardy in USDA zones 4 to 8 and can be propagated by cuttings or by layering. Pruning should be done after flowering to maintain its shape and promote new growth.

USES

Syringa josikaea is primarily grown as an ornamental plant for its beautiful flowers and attractive bark. It is a popular choice for hedges, borders, and specimen plants. The flowers can also be cut and used in floral arrangements.

SYRINGA OBLATA - A CHINESE NATIVE LILAC WITH FRAGRANT PALE PINK OR WHITE FLOWERS

DESCRIPTION

Syringa oblata, commonly known as the early lilac, is a deciduous shrub that typically grows up to 10 feet tall. It has dark green leaves and produces fragrant clusters of pale pink or white flowers in the early spring, before many other lilac species have bloomed. The plant is known for its rounded growth habit and attractive bark.

ORIGIN AND DISTRIBUTION

Syringa oblata is native to China and Korea, and has been cultivated for its ornamental value. It can be found growing in gardens and landscapes throughout North America and Europe.

CULTIVATION

The early lilac prefers full sun to partial shade and well-drained soil. It is hardy in USDA zones 4 to 7 and can be propagated by cuttings or by layering. Pruning should be done after flowering to maintain its shape and promote new growth.

USES

Syringa oblata is primarily grown as an ornamental plant for its beautiful early spring flowers and attractive bark. It is a popular choice for hedges, borders, and specimen plants. The flowers can also be cut and used in floral arrangements.

SYRINGA X PRESTONIAE - A HYBRID LILAC WITH PINK, LAVENDER, OR WHITE FLOWERS

DESCRIPTION

Syringa x prestoniae, commonly known as Preston lilac, is a deciduous shrub that can grow up to 10 feet tall. It has dark green leaves and produces clusters of fragrant flowers in shades of pink, lavender, or white in the late spring to early summer. The plant is known for its upright growth habit and attractive bark.

ORIGIN AND DISTRIBUTION

Syringa x prestoniae is a hybrid of Syringa villosa and Syringa reflexa. It was developed by Isabella Preston, a Canadian plant breeder, in the early 20th century. The plant has been cultivated for its ornamental value and can be found growing in gardens and landscapes throughout North America and Europe.

CULTIVATION

The Preston lilac prefers full sun to partial shade and well-drained soil. It is hardy in USDA zones 3 to 7 and can be propagated by cuttings or by layering. Pruning should be done after flowering to maintain its shape and promote new growth.

USES

Syringa x prestoniae is primarily grown as an ornamental plant for its beautiful flowers and attractive bark. It is a popular choice for hedges, borders, and specimen plants. The flowers can also be cut and used in floral arrangements.

SYRINGA RETICULATA - A JAPANESE NATIVE LILAC WITH FRAGRANT WHITE FLOWERS

DESCRIPTION

Syringa reticulata, commonly known as the Japanese tree lilac, is a deciduous tree that can grow up to 40 feet tall. It has dark green leaves and produces large clusters of fragrant white flowers in early summer. The plant is known for its upright growth habit and attractive bark.

ORIGIN AND DISTRIBUTION

Syringa reticulata is native to Japan and has been cultivated for its ornamental value. It can be found growing in gardens and landscapes throughout North America and Europe.

CULTIVATION

The Japanese tree lilac prefers full sun to partial shade and well-drained soil. It is hardy in USDA zones 4 to 7 and can be propagated by seed or by grafting. Pruning should be done in the winter or early spring to maintain its shape and promote new growth.

USES

Syringa reticulata is primarily grown as an ornamental tree for its beautiful flowers and attractive bark. It is a popular choice for parks, gardens, and along streets and sidewalks. The flowers can also be cut and used in floral arrangements.

SYRINGA PERSICA - A PERSIAN NATIVE LILAC WITH PALE PINK OR LILAC FLOWERS

DESCRIPTION

Syringa persica, commonly known as the Persian lilac, is a deciduous shrub that can grow up to 10 feet tall. It has narrow, lance-shaped leaves and produces clusters of pale pink or lilac flowers in late spring or early summer. The plant is known for its delicate appearance and sweet fragrance.

ORIGIN AND DISTRIBUTION

Syringa persica is native to Iran and Iraq, but has been widely cultivated for its ornamental value. It can be found growing in gardens and landscapes throughout North America and Europe.

CULTIVATION

The Persian lilac prefers full sun to partial shade and well-drained soil. It is hardy in USDA zones 3 to 7 and can be propagated by seed or by cuttings. Pruning should be done in the winter or early spring to maintain its shape and promote new growth.

USES

Syringa persica is primarily grown as an ornamental shrub for its beautiful flowers and sweet fragrance. It is a popular choice for small gardens, borders, and along pathways. The flowers can also be cut and used in floral arrangements.

SYRINGA PROTOLACINIATA - A CHINESE NATIVE LILAC WITH PALE PINK OR WHITE FLOWERS

DESCRIPTION

Syringa protolaciniata, commonly known as the early lilac, is a deciduous shrub that can grow up to 10 feet tall. It has oval-shaped leaves and produces clusters of pale pink or white flowers in early spring. The plant is known for its early blooming and fragrant flowers.

ORIGIN AND DISTRIBUTION

Syringa protolaciniata is native to China and has been widely cultivated for its ornamental value. It can be found growing in gardens and landscapes throughout North America and Europe.

CULTIVATION

The early lilac prefers full sun to partial shade and well-drained soil. It is hardy in USDA zones 3 to 7 and can be propagated by seed or by cuttings. Pruning should be done immediately after flowering to maintain its shape and promote new growth.

USES

Syringa protolaciniata is primarily grown as an ornamental shrub for its early blooming and fragrant flowers. It is a popular choice for small gardens, borders, and along pathways. The flowers can also be cut and used in floral arrangements.

SYRINGA TOMENTELLA - A CHINESE NATIVE LILAC WITH PALE LAVENDER-PINK FLOWERS

DESCRIPTION

Syringa tomentella, also known as the Yunnan lilac, is a deciduous shrub that can grow up to 10 feet tall. It has dark green, glossy leaves that are tinged with purple in the fall. In the spring, the plant produces clusters of fragrant, pale lavender-pink flowers that attract pollinators such as bees and butterflies.

ORIGIN AND DISTRIBUTION

Syringa tomentella is native to China and can be found growing in the Yunnan Province at elevations between 6,000 and 10,000 feet. It has also been introduced to other parts of the world, including North America and Europe.

CULTIVATION

The Yunnan lilac prefers full sun to partial shade and well-drained soil. It is hardy in USDA zones 7 to 9 and can be propagated by seed or by cuttings. Pruning should be done after flowering to maintain its shape and promote new growth.

USES

Syringa tomentella is primarily grown as an ornamental shrub for its fragrant flowers and attractive foliage. It is a popular choice for gardens, borders, and as a specimen plant. The flowers can also be cut and used in floral arrangements.

SYRINGA X LACINIATA - A HYBRID LILAC WITH DEEP PURPLE FLOWERS

DESCRIPTION

Syringa x laciniata, also known as the cutleaf lilac, is a deciduous shrub that can reach a height of up to 12 feet. It has dark green, deeply cut leaves that give it a delicate and lacy appearance. In the late spring, it produces clusters of fragrant, deep purple flowers that attract pollinators such as bees and butterflies.

ORIGIN AND DISTRIBUTION

Syringa x laciniata is a hybrid of Syringa vulgaris and Syringa protolaciniata. It was first developed in France in the 19th century. It is now grown in many parts of the world, including North America and Europe.

CULTIVATION

The cutleaf lilac prefers full sun to partial shade and well-drained soil. It is hardy in USDA zones 3 to 7 and can be propagated by seed or by cuttings. Pruning should be done after flowering to maintain its shape and promote new growth.

USES

Syringa x laciniata is primarily grown as an ornamental shrub for its fragrant flowers and attractive foliage. It is a popular choice for gardens, borders, and as a specimen plant. The flowers can also be cut and used in floral arrangements. Its delicate foliage also makes it a good choice for adding texture and interest to mixed borders or as a focal point in a landscape design.

SYRINGA MICROPHYLLA - A HIMALAYAN NATIVE LILAC WITH FRAGRANT PINK OR RED FLOWERS

DESCRIPTION

Syringa microphylla, commonly known as the littleleaf lilac, is a deciduous shrub that typically grows to a height of 6-10 feet and a spread of 8-12 feet. Its leaves are small, about 1 inch long, and glossy. In late spring to early summer, it produces clusters of fragrant, pink or red flowers that are about 3-4 inches long.

ORIGIN AND DISTRIBUTION

Syringa microphylla is native to the Himalayas, from Nepal to China. It has been cultivated in Europe and North America since the 19th century.

CULTIVATION

The littleleaf lilac prefers full sun to partial shade and well-drained soil. It is hardy in USDA zones 4 to 7. It can be propagated by seed or by cuttings. Pruning should be done after flowering to maintain its shape and promote new growth.

USES

Syringa microphylla is primarily grown as an ornamental shrub for its fragrant flowers and attractive foliage. It is a popular choice for small gardens or as a specimen plant. It can also be used for hedges or as a border plant. The flowers can be cut and used in floral arrangements.

SYRINGA KOMAROWII

OVERVIEW

Syringa komarowii, commonly known as the Komarov lilac, is a deciduous shrub species of the genus Syringa and is native to Japan, Korea, and China. It grows up to 3 meters tall and produces fragrant white or pale pink flowers in late spring or early summer. The flowers are borne in panicles, which are up to 25 cm long and composed of numerous individual blooms.

CHARACTERISTICS

- Leaves: Dark green, ovate or elliptic, 2-5 cm long, and turn yellow in fall.
- Flowers: Fragrant, white or pale pink, tubular, and up to 1 cm long. They bloom in late spring or early summer.
- Fruit: Brown, ovoid, and up to 1 cm long.
- Bark: Brown-gray and fissured.
- Growth: Slow-growing, up to 3 meters tall and wide.

CULTIVATION

Syringa komarowii prefers well-drained soils and partial shade to full sun. It is drought-tolerant and can grow in various soil types, including sandy, loamy, and clay soils. The shrub is hardy and can withstand temperatures as low as -25°C. Pruning is not necessary but can be done to maintain its shape.

DESCRIPTION

Syringa wolfii is a deciduous shrub species of the Oleaceae family, commonly known as the Wolf lilac. It is native to China and can grow up to 6 feet in height and spread. The leaves are lance-shaped, dark green, and slightly hairy. The flowers are fragrant, white, or pale pink in color, and appear in clusters in late spring to early summer.

CULTIVATION

Syringa wolfii is hardy and adaptable to various soil types, but prefers well-drained soil and full sunlight. It is resistant to diseases and pests and can grow in USDA hardiness zones 3 to 7. Pruning is recommended after flowering to maintain its shape and promote new growth.

USES

Syringa wolfii is primarily used as an ornamental plant in gardens, parks, and landscapes. Its fragrant flowers and attractive foliage make it a popular choice for borders, hedges, and mixed shrubbery. It can also be grown as a bonsai tree and used in cut flower arrangements.

SYRINGA EMODI - OVERVIEW

Syringa emodi, also known as the Himalayan lilac, is a deciduous shrub or small tree that is native to the Himalayan region of Asia. It can grow up to 5 meters tall and has a rounded, spreading habit. The leaves are dark green, glossy, and ovate in shape, growing up to 15 cm long. In spring, it produces clusters of fragrant, tubular flowers that are white or pale pink in color.

HABITAT AND CULTIVATION

Syringa emodi is typically found growing in forested areas and on slopes at elevations of 1,500 to 3,000 meters. It is well-suited to temperate climates and can tolerate some drought conditions. It prefers well-draining soils and full to partial sun exposure.

As an ornamental plant, Syringa emodi is often grown for its attractive flowers and foliage. It can be propagated from seed or cuttings and is relatively low-maintenance once established.

USES

In addition to its ornamental value, Syringa emodi has been used in traditional medicine for a variety of purposes. The bark and leaves have been used to treat skin conditions, fever, and respiratory ailments. The wood is also valued for its hardness and durability, and has been used in construction and for making furniture and tools.

SYRINGA PATENS - OVERVIEW

Syringa patens, commonly known as Siberian lilac, is a deciduous shrub belonging to the olive family. It is native to eastern Siberia and northern China and is widely cultivated as an ornamental plant for its attractive flowers and foliage.

APPEARANCE

The shrub grows up to 4-8 feet tall and spreads up to 5-7 feet wide. It has a dense, upright, and rounded habit. The leaves are simple, ovate, and dark green in color, measuring 2-5 inches long. The flowers are produced in large, showy panicles that emerge in late spring to early summer. The individual flowers are small and tubular, measuring about ½ inch long, and are arranged in clusters of 10-20 per panicle. The flowers are usually blue-violet in color, but some cultivars may have lighter or darker shades of blue or purple. They are highly fragrant and attract bees, butterflies, and hummingbirds.

CULTIVATION

Syringa patens is an easy-to-grow plant that prefers full sun to partial shade and well-drained soil. It is tolerant of a wide range of soil types, including sandy, loamy, and clay soils. The plant has moderate water needs and requires regular watering during the growing season. It is generally disease-resistant and not prone to pests, but may occasionally suffer from powdery mildew or leaf spot. Pruning is recommended immediately after flowering to maintain its shape and promote healthy growth.

USES

Syringa patens is a popular ornamental plant for gardens and landscapes. It is often used as a specimen plant, hedge, or screen. The plant's fragrant flowers and foliage make it an excellent choice for cut flowers or as a natural air freshener. Its hardiness and adaptability also make it a good choice for urban and suburban landscapes.

SYRINGA YUNNANENSIS - CHINESE NATIVE LILAC

OVERVIEW:

Syringa yunnanensis, also known as Yunnan lilac, is a deciduous shrub that is native to southwestern China. It is part of the olive family and is commonly grown for its beautiful pink or purple flowers that bloom in the late spring or early summer.

PHYSICAL DESCRIPTION:

The Yunnan lilac grows up to 3-4 meters tall and wide, and has a dense, bushy habit. Its leaves are oval-shaped, dark green in color, and up to 10 cm long. The flowers are produced in large clusters, with each individual flower being tubular in shape and around 2.5-3 cm long. They have four petals and come in shades of pink or purple, with a delicate fragrance.

CULTIVATION:

Syringa yunnanensis is a hardy plant that can tolerate a wide range of soil types and conditions, but it prefers well-draining soil and a sunny or partially shaded location. It is best propagated by softwood cuttings taken in the early summer and should be pruned after flowering to maintain its shape and promote new growth. Yunnan lilac is a popular ornamental plant in gardens and parks, and its flowers are also used for cut arrangements.

SYRINGA X CHINENSIS

OVERVIEW

Syringa x chinensis is a hybrid lilac that is believed to have been created in the 18th century by crossing Syringa vulgaris with other species native to China. It is a deciduous shrub that typically grows to a height of 10-15 feet, with a spread of 8-12 feet. The plant produces fragrant white or pale pink flowers in late spring or early summer, which are arranged in large panicles.

APPEARANCE

The leaves of Syringa x chinensis are dark green and slightly glossy, and typically have a heart-shaped base. The flowers are tubular and have a delicate fragrance. They are usually white or pale pink in color, and are arranged in panicles that can be up to 10 inches long.

CULTIVATION

Syringa x chinensis prefers well-drained soils and full sun or partial shade. It is tolerant of a wide range of soil types, including loam, sand, and clay. The plant is hardy in USDA zones 3-8, and can tolerate temperatures as low as -40°F. It is relatively easy to grow and maintain, and is often used as a specimen plant in gardens and landscapes.

SYRINGA X JOSIFLEXA - OVERVIEW

DESCRIPTION

Syringa x josiflexa is a hybrid lilac that results from crossing Syringa vulgaris with Syringa x chinensis. It is a deciduous shrub that grows up to 10 feet tall and wide. The leaves are dark green and heart-shaped. The flowers bloom in late spring to early summer and are highly fragrant. The flowers can be pink or purple, and the panicles can reach up to 12 inches long.

CULTIVATION

Syringa x josiflexa prefers full sun and well-drained soil. It is tolerant of a wide range of soil types and pH levels. Regular watering is needed for young plants, but mature plants are drought-tolerant. Pruning should be done immediately after flowering to avoid cutting off next year's flower buds.

USES

Syringa x josiflexa is often used as a specimen plant in landscapes, but can also be used in mixed borders or as a hedge. The highly fragrant flowers are a popular choice for cut flower arrangements. The shrub attracts bees, butterflies, and other pollinators to the garden.

SYRINGA X PERSICIFOLIA

OVERVIEW

Syringa x persicifolia is a hybrid lilac resulting from a cross between Syringa reflexa and Syringa laciniata. It is a deciduous shrub that typically grows to a height of 8-10 feet, with a spread of 6-8 feet. The leaves are dark green, glossy, and lance-shaped, with a length of 2-4 inches. The flowers are fragrant, white or pale pink, and appear in late spring to early summer. They are arranged in panicles, with each panicle containing numerous individual blooms.

USES

Syringa x persicifolia is commonly grown as an ornamental shrub in gardens and landscapes. Its fragrant flowers and attractive foliage make it a popular choice for borders, hedges, and specimen plantings. It is also often used in cut flower arrangements.

CULTIVATION

Syringa x persicifolia prefers full sun to partial shade and well-drained, fertile soil. It is generally easy to grow and relatively low maintenance. Pruning should be done after flowering to promote bushiness and maintain a desirable shape. It is hardy in USDA zones 3-7.

SYRINGA KOMAROVII SUBSP. REFLEXA

OVERVIEW

Syringa komarovii subsp. reflexa, commonly known as reflexed lilac, is a subspecies of Syringa komarovii, a Japanese native lilac. It is a deciduous shrub or small tree that typically grows up to 6 meters tall. The flowers are pale pink or white and are borne in clusters that appear in late spring to early summer. It is valued for its fragrant blooms and attractive foliage.

CULTIVATION

Syringa komarovii subsp. reflexa is a hardy plant that grows best in well-drained soils in full sun to partial shade. It is tolerant of drought and pollution and is suitable for growing in urban environments. It can be propagated by seeds or cuttings and is commonly used as an ornamental plant in gardens and parks.

USES

The fragrant flowers of Syringa komarovii subsp. reflexa are used for making perfumes and as a flavoring agent in teas and other beverages. The plant is also used in traditional medicine for its antipyretic and anti-inflammatory properties.

OVERVIEW OF SYRINGA VILLOSA

INTRODUCTION

Syringa villosa, commonly known as the Late Lilac, is a deciduous shrub that is native to China. It belongs to the olive family (Oleaceae) and is related to other popular garden plants such as jasmine and olive trees. The plant is prized for its beautiful fragrant flowers that bloom in late spring to early summer.

APPEARANCE

The plant grows up to 10 feet tall and 8 feet wide, and has a rounded shape. The leaves are dark green and glossy, and grow up to 5 inches long. The flowers are pale pink or white, and grow in large panicles up to 8 inches long. The blooms are highly fragrant and attract bees and butterflies to the garden.

CULTIVATION

Syringa villosa prefers full sun to partial shade and well-drained soil. It is hardy in USDA zones 3 to 7 and can withstand cold temperatures and harsh winters. The plant is low maintenance and can be pruned after flowering to maintain its shape and size. Propagation can be done through seed or cuttings.

USES

Syringa villosa is a popular ornamental plant for gardens and landscapes due to its attractive foliage and fragrant flowers. It is often used as a specimen plant, hedge or border plant, and can also be planted in containers. The flowers are often used in cut flower arrangements and can be enjoyed indoors as well.

SYRINGA X NANCEIAE

OVERVIEW

Syringa x nanceiae is a hybrid lilac that originated from a cross between Syringa oblata and Syringa vulgaris. It is a deciduous shrub that can reach up to 10 feet in height and spread. The foliage is dark green and the flowers are highly fragrant, appearing in spring and early summer. The flowers are typically white or pale pink and are arranged in panicles.

HISTORY AND CULTIVATION

Syringa x nanceiae was first developed in the United States by Dr. Donald Egolf at the United States National Arboretum in Washington, D.C. It was named after Dr. Elwin R. Orton's wife, Nancy. The plant is hardy and easy to grow, and can tolerate a wide range of soil types. It prefers full sun to partial shade and requires regular watering.

USES

Syringa x nanceiae is often grown as an ornamental shrub in gardens and parks. Its highly fragrant flowers make it a popular choice for cut flowers and as a source of essential oil. The plant is also used in traditional medicine to treat a variety of ailments.

SYRINGA EMEROIDES

Syringa emeroides, commonly known as Chinese lilac, is a deciduous shrub or small tree native to China. It can grow up to 4 meters in height and has an upright, spreading habit. The leaves are dark green and glossy, and the bark is brown and furrowed.

The flowers are fragrant and appear in mid- to late spring. They are small, measuring about 1 cm in diameter, and are typically white or pale pink. The flowers are borne in large clusters, or panicles, which can be up to 20 cm long.

Chinese lilac is a popular ornamental plant in gardens and parks, valued for its attractive flowers and foliage. It is also used as a cut flower in floral arrangements.

SYRINGA X HYBRIDA

Syringa x hybrida, also known as hybrid lilac, is a hybrid of several lilac species, including Syringa vulgaris and Syringa persica. It is a deciduous shrub that can grow up to 6 meters tall and 4 meters wide. The leaves are green and heart-shaped, and the flowers are fragrant and appear in spring or early summer in shades of pink or white. The plant is often used as an ornamental shrub in gardens and parks due to its attractive appearance and lovely scent.

HISTORY

The first hybrid lilac was created by crossing Syringa vulgaris and Syringa oblata in 1889 by Victor Lemoine, a French nurseryman. Since then, many other hybrids have been developed, including Syringa x hybrida, which is a cross between Syringa vulgaris and Syringa persica.

CULTIVATION

Syringa x hybrida is a hardy plant that can tolerate a wide range of soil types and climatic conditions. It prefers full sun or partial shade and well-drained soil. The plant should be watered regularly during dry periods and pruned after flowering to maintain its shape and promote healthy growth. Propagation can be done by taking softwood cuttings in early summer or by layering in autumn.

USES

Syringa x hybrida is primarily used as an ornamental plant in gardens and parks due to its beautiful flowers and lovely fragrance. The flowers can also be used in floral arrangements. In traditional medicine, various parts of the plant are used for their medicinal properties, including treating fever, inflammation, and pain.

SYRINGA AFGHANICA

OVERVIEW

Syringa afghanica, also known as Afghan lilac, is a deciduous shrub that is native to Afghanistan. It is a member of the olive family, and it typically grows to a height of 3-4 meters. Afghan lilac has an upright growth habit and a dense, bushy form.

APPEARANCE

The leaves of Syringa afghanica are dark green and elongated, measuring up to 10 cm in length. The flowers are fragrant and can be white, pale pink, or lilac in color. They are produced in large clusters in late spring to early summer and attract butterflies and bees.

CULTIVATION

Syringa afghanica is relatively easy to grow and prefers well-draining soil in full sun to partial shade. It is hardy to USDA zones 6-9 and can tolerate drought conditions once established. Pruning should be done after flowering to encourage a compact shape and to remove any dead or diseased wood.

USES

Syringa afghanica is commonly grown as an ornamental shrub in gardens and parks. Its fragrant flowers make it a popular choice for cut flower arrangements. In traditional

Afghan medicine, the leaves and bark of the plant have been used to treat a variety of ailments, including rheumatism, skin diseases, and fever.

SYRINGA X DIVERSIFOLIA

OVERVIEW

Syringa x diversifolia is a hybrid lilac that is believed to be a cross between Syringa vulgaris and Syringa oblata. It is also known as the Himalayan lilac or the Himalayan hybrid lilac. The plant produces fragrant pink or white flowers that bloom in late spring or early summer. The leaves of the plant are typically dark green and ovate in shape, and the bark is gray or brown and can be smooth or slightly rough.

GROWING CONDITIONS

Syringa x diversifolia prefers well-drained soil and full sun to partial shade. It can tolerate a wide range of soil types, including clay and sand, and is relatively drought-tolerant once established. The plant is hardy in USDA zones 3 to 7.

CARE

Pruning is generally not necessary for Syringa x diversifolia, but it can be done after the plant has finished blooming if desired. Fertilization is also not usually necessary, but a slow-release fertilizer can be applied in early spring if desired.

USES

Syringa x diversifolia is often used as an ornamental shrub in gardens and landscapes. The fragrant flowers make it an attractive choice for planting near patios, decks, or other outdoor living spaces. The plant can also be used as a hedge or border plant, or as a specimen plant in a mixed border.

SYRINGA KOMAROVII - JAPANESE NATIVE LILAC

OVERVIEW

Syringa komarovii is a species of lilac native to Japan. It is a deciduous shrub that typically grows to a height of 1-3 meters. The leaves are ovate or elliptic and measure 5-15 centimeters in length. The flowers of Syringa komarovii are white or pale pink, and they bloom in late spring to early summer. The flowers are fragrant and attract bees, butterflies, and other pollinators. After flowering, the shrub produces small brown capsules that contain the seeds.

CULTIVATION

Syringa komarovii prefers full sun to partial shade and well-drained soil. It is drought tolerant once established but benefits from regular watering during dry spells. The shrub is generally easy to grow and is relatively pest and disease resistant. Pruning is recommended after flowering to maintain a compact shape and encourage new growth.

USES

Syringa komarovii is commonly grown as an ornamental plant in gardens and parks. Its fragrant flowers and attractive foliage make it a popular choice for landscaping. The shrub is also used in traditional medicine in Japan and China, where it is believed to have various health benefits.

Made in United States
Troutdale, OR
06/10/2023

10532713R00033